# 12 DAYS of SOUTHERN CHRISTMAS

WRITTEN BY KELLY KAZEK ✳ ILLUSTRATED BY JAN SHADE BEACH

Printed in Canada
First edition September 2023
ISBN: 978-1-57571-912-2
(hardback)

Designer: Abby Williams
abbywilliamsdesign.com

**W**ho, really, has a need for 10 lords a'leaping? What does that even mean? While it's possible a lord might *leap*, it seems highly unlikely he would *a'leap*, or that ten would a'leap at one time ... or even be in the same house ... wait, unless it was the House of Lords. And don't get us started on maids a'milking.

We admit we wouldn't turn up our noses at five golden rings but much of the traditional song "The 12 Days of Christmas" is not relatable to the average person. Perhaps that's because it was written in the eighteenth century, back when having a partridge in a pear tree equaled dinner and dessert.

So why is this song a beloved, or at least tolerated, classic?

It turns out the song was once a type of game, back before TV and internet and, you know, fun.

The verses first appeared in a 1780 children's book called *Mirth With-out Mischief,* according to History.com.

Historians believe it was a memory-and-forfeits game, in which players would see how many verses they could recall.

When players forgot the lyrics, they would "forfeit" a kiss or other prize to their opponent.

Although the items mentioned in the song are not religious, the 12 Days of Christmas is a period of time in Christian theology. It spans from the day after Christmas through Epiphany on January 6, which was the amount of time between the birth of Christ and the arrival of the wise men.

A lot has changed since the poem/carol first appeared, including many things about Southern culture. Here in the South, Christmas is a little different.

For starters, it's hot here. Sometimes, even in December.

And then there's the food – we're crazy for any casserole made with a can of cream-of-something soup and we love to see what kinds of things we can suspend in gelatin.

To make the carol more relatable to folks in our neck of the woods, we wrote the *Twelve Days of Southern Christmas*, just for y'all.

We changed "my true love" to "my mama," because, well, mama is the heart of everything. (We're not the first to do this, actually. At times throughout history, mothers have replaced "true loves" as the gift givers.)

Now, get the tune going in your head ... ready? Go.

# ON THE

## FIRST

### DAY OF CHRISTMAS,

*my mama gave to me ...*

BREAD AND MILK IN
CASE OF A STORM.

A Southern mama would be remiss if she didn't help her family prepare for a storm. It could be a snowstorm, tornado or hurricane, depending on which part of the South you're in but, in any case, the correct response to the forecast is to run to the store to buy bread and milk. No one knows why, really, although some people theorize mamas like to have extra bread sacks on hand to wrap around the children's feet when they play in the snow. Water-proofing, y'all. It's not like we own snow boots.

# ON THE

# SECOND

 ## DAY OF CHRISTMAS,

*my mama gave to me ...*

# 2 CAST-IRON SKILLETS ...

Because one is not enough ... and she sure doesn't want you borrowing hers. And if you ever, ever, put one in the dishwasher, she'll take them both away and revoke your Southern card.

... AND BREAD AND MILK
IN CASE OF A STORM.

# ON THE

# THIRD

## DAY OF CHRISTMAS,

*my mama gave to me ...*

3 FRONT-PORCH ROCKERS ...

Just enough so you can spend time with
mama'n'em, shooting the breeze, sipping
iced tea and *not* gossiping about anyone.
God love 'em.

**2** CAST-IRON SKILLETS,

AND BREAD AND MILK
IN CASE OF A STORM.

# ON THE
# FOURTH
## DAY OF CHRISTMAS,

*my mama gave to me ...*

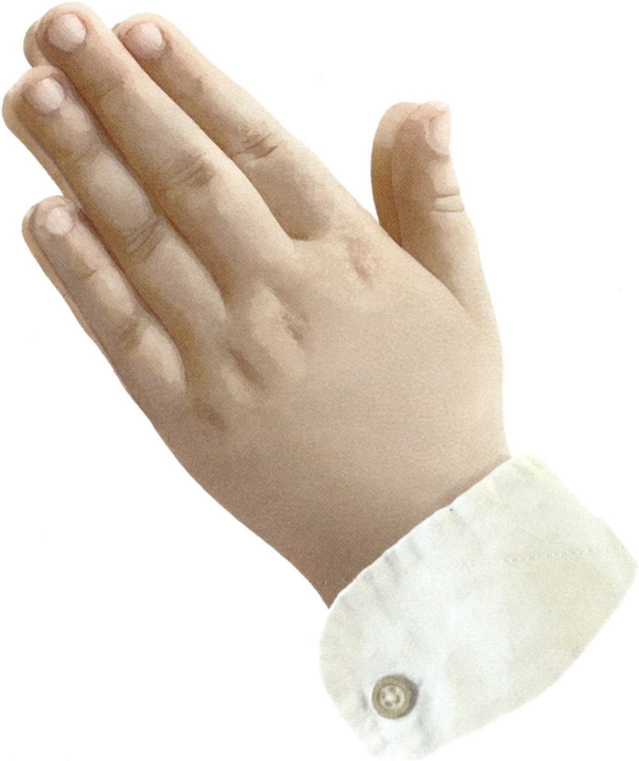

# 4 MINUTES OF BLESSINGS ...

... and 14 cousins waiting for the "amen" so they
can fill their plates with five kinds of casseroles
and then sit around and complain they ate
too much ... and then do it all again.

**3** FRONT-PORCH ROCKERS,

**2** CAST-IRON SKILLETS,

 AND BREAD AND MILK
IN CASE OF A STORM.

# ON THE

# FIFTH

 DAY OF CHRISTMAS,

*my mama gave to me ...*

RECIPE  Pecan Pie
1 cup white sugar
3 tbsp brown sugar
1 cup corn syrup
3/3 tsp - vanilla
1/3 cup melted butter
3 eggs, beaten
1 heaping cup of pecans

5. PECAN PIES ...

... made from Great-Grandmother's recipe, which, no matter how closely you follow, never results in a pie as yummy as hers. Because she used love and fairy dust.

**4** MINUTES OF BLESSING,

**3** FRONT-PORCH ROCKERS,

**2** CAST-IRON SKILLETS,

AND BREAD AND MILK
IN CASE OF A STORM.

# ON THE

## SIXTH

### DAY OF CHRISTMAS,

*my mama gave to me ...*

**6**

**BOWL-GAME TICKETS ...**

On the 50-yard line because we know at least one
of our favorite teams will be playing.

Be sure they include those little padded seats —
those bleachers are *hard*, y'all.

**5** PECAN PIES,

**4** MINUTES OF BLESSING,

**3** FRONT-PORCH ROCKERS,

**2** CAST-IRON SKILLETS,

AND BREAD AND MILK
IN CASE OF A STORM.

ON THE

# SEVENTH

## DAY OF CHRISTMAS,

*my mama gave to me ...*

 **7** HANDWRITTEN RECIPES ..

**Recipe**

Lane Cake

3 1/4 cups cake flour sifted
1 cup butter
2 cups granulated sugar
8 eggs
1 cup milk
1 cup seedless raisins
3 cups bourbon
2 tsp. vanilla

Directions on back →

**RECIPE** Grandma's Banana Pudding

1 box hem...        1 Whisk pudding mix. Eagle Brand milk
1 box va...          ...ld milk together till smooth
1 can s...           ...d place a layer of
5 cups...            ...h. Top
1 box...
2...

**RECIPE** Pecan Pie

1 cup white sugar
3 tbsp brown sugar
1 cup corn syrup
3/4 tsp. vanilla
1/3 cup melted butter
3 eggs beaten
1 heaping cup of pecans

These recipes are worth their weight in buttermilk biscuits. They may be encrusted in unidentifiable splotches and splashes of vanilla extract but they are also touched with bits of MeeMaw's love and her culinary magic.

6 BOWL-GAME TICKETS,

5 PECAN PIES,

4 MINUTES OF BLESSING,

3 FRONT-PORCH ROCKERS,

2 CAST-IRON SKILLETS,

AND BREAD AND MILK
IN CASE OF A STORM.

# ON THE

# EIGHTH

## DAY OF CHRISTMAS,

*my mama gave to me ...*

 "BLESS YOUR HEARTS ..."

One for every day of the week, plus one for emergencies.

It's holiday season — you're gonna need it.

**7** HANDWRITTEN RECIPES,

**6** BOWL-GAME TICKETS,

**5** PECAN PIES,

**4** MINUTES OF BLESSING,

**3** FRONT-PORCH ROCKERS,

**2** CAST-IRON SKILLETS,

AND BREAD AND MILK
IN CASE OF A STORM.

# ON THE

# NINTH

## DAY OF CHRISTMAS,

*my mama gave to me ...*

WARM WISHES

9 DURAFLAME LOGS ...

... with the air-conditioning turned on because it's too dadburned hot outside for a fire but it's the holiday season and mama wanted one so ...

**8** "BLESS YOUR HEARTS,"

**7** HANDWRITTEN RECIPES,

**6** BOWL-GAME TICKETS,

**5** PECAN PIES,

4 MINUTES OF BLESSING,

3 FRONT-PORCH ROCKERS,

2 CAST-IRON SKILLETS,

AND BREAD AND MILK
IN CASE OF A STORM.

# ON THE

# TENTH

## DAY OF CHRISTMAS,

*my mama gave to me ...*

10 GALLONS OF SWEET TEA ...

And maybe one gallon of unsweetened for the out-of-towners, although you may as well use the instant stuff with fake lemon if you're going to do that.

**9** DURAFLAME LOGS,

**8** "BLESS YOUR HEARTS,"

**7** HANDWRITTEN RECIPES,

**6** BOWL-GAME TICKETS,

**5** PECAN PIES,

**4** MINUTES OF BLESSING,

**3** FRONT-PORCH ROCKERS,

**2** CAST-IRON SKILLETS,

 AND BREAD AND MILK IN CASE OF A STORM.

# ON THE

# ELEVENTH

 DAY OF CHRISTMAS,

*my mama gave to me ...*

# 11 BUTTERMILK BISCUITS ...

Along with a repurposed Cool Whip
tub filled with gravy because they're just
so much better with the gravy.

**10** GALLONS OF SWEET TEA,

**9** DURAFLAME LOGS,

**8** "BLESS YOUR HEARTS,"

**7** HANDWRITTEN RECIPES,

**6** BOWL-GAME TICKETS,

**5** PECAN PIES,

**4** MINUTES OF BLESSING,

**3** FRONT-PORCH ROCKERS,

**2** CAST-IRON SKILLETS,

 AND BREAD AND MILK
IN CASE OF A STORM.

# ON THE

# TWELFTH

 ## DAY OF CHRISTMAS,

*my mama gave to me ...*

**12 DEVILED EGGS ...**

After all, that's the perfect amount for your brand-new deviled egg platter that was gifted to you by Aunt Ella Dean so you will have it when you come to her next potluck. She's tired of your cheap plastic containers, if you wanna know the truth about it.

11 BUTTERMILK BISCUITS,

10 GALLONS OF SWEET TEA,

9 DURAFLAME LOGS,

8 "BLESS YOUR HEARTS,"

7 HANDWRITTEN RECIPES,

6 BOWL-GAME TICKETS,

**5** PECAN PIES,

**4** MINUTES OF BLESSING,

**3** FRONT-PORCH ROCKERS,

**2** CAST-IRON SKILLETS,

AND BREAD AND MILK
IN CASE OF A STORM.

MERRY CHRISTMAS Y'ALL

AND HAPPY NEW YEAR!
THANKS FOR SINGING ALONG.

## ABOUT THE AUTHOR

Kelly Kazek is an award-winning journalist and author who writes about Southern culture. She is the author of numerous children's picture books for It's a Southern Thing, including *Y is for Y'all*, as well as *Southern Handbook: How to Quit Being Ugly and Act Like Somebody*, two collections of humorous essays, and numerous books of regional history. She lives near Huntsville, Alabama. Contact her at kkazek@southernthing.com.

## ABOUT THE ILLUSTRATOR

In addition to this book, Jan Shade Beach has illustrated the picture book *The Sun Has Gone to Bed* for It's a Southern Thing. She is also an accomplished commercial artist and designer who has created a myriad of licensed products ranging from greeting cards, rugs, prints, gift bags/boxes, giftware, fabric, and more.

She is best known for creating holiday characters for top-selling lines for retailers such as Kohl's, Target, Yankee Candle, Wal-Mart, and more. She works from her home studio near Huntsville, Alabama.

**Don't miss these other Southern-themed books
from It's a Southern Thing!**

The *Southern Thesaurus*, all about our colorful phrases and language;
The *Southern Handbook*, a handy guide for any Southerner or wannabe Southerner;
*100 Southern Ways to Say I Love You*, this small, colorful book makes the perfect
gift; *Just Like Mama Used to Say*, a book of sayings and remedies from Southern
mothers (a companion to our best-selling game of the same name.)
Don't miss our full line of Southern-themed children's books!

store.southernthing.com